Heart in my Boots

by Roy Crompton
with cartoons by Bob Park

Tales from the life of a Birmingham policeman in the 1950's, 60's and 70's; strange and hilarious. This is *real* police work; not stakeouts, shootouts and car chases, but ferocious dogs, corpses in coffins, stray donkeys and lost tailor's dummies.

****
QuercuS
John Roberts
8 Hillside Close, Bartley Green
Birmingham B32 4LT
****

Heart in my Boots
by Roy Crompton
with cartoons by Bob Park

ISBN 1 898136 10 6

First Published 1996

The Author

Roy Crompton was born at Ormskirk, Lancashire in 1929, son of Harold, an LMS Railway clerk. In 1939 his father moved to Ipstones on the moors near Leek, from where Roy travelled to Burslem Junior Technical College for his secondary education. Later he attended Stoke on Trent Technical College, followed by National Service between 1947 and 1949 in the RAF Police.

After discharge he applied for a job with the Stoke on Trent police, but as he says in his *Introduction,* he was a fraction short of inches, so in 1950 joined the Birmingham force. Roy retired from the police in 1977 but worked until 1986 as a DSS security guard. Trying to contain violence and bad behaviour without the power to deal with it became more stressful than policing and made Roy unwell, so at last he took final retirement.

These stories are recollections of his working life which were written after finishing with work, when Roy took an evening course in Creative Writing at Northfield Adult Education Centre. He says they were written partly as a therapy and helped him recover from the nervous strain of security work. We should add that he has written a great many more - this book is a small selection.

The title *Heart in my Boots* would probably be apt for any policeman, but in Roy's case it also comes from a lifelong love of Gilbert & Sullivan operas. The phrase comes from the Policeman's Song in *The Pirates of Penzance.* His father was lead tenor in an amateur company and the leading voices would often rehearse at the Crompton home. At the age of 22 months he heard *The Mikado* from near the stage on his mother's knee. The words and music of G & S have always been part of his life, and he sometimes saw the people he met as characters in the operas.

Roy now lives with wife Doreen and son Jeffrey in Selly Oak, and often sees his daughters Janice and Hazel, who have (so far) given him five grandchildren. He still enjoys G and S and a wide range of classical and modern music, he supports the Royal National Lifeboat Institution and Birmingham Children's Hospice. When they can get away the Cromptons love to stay in their caravan on the Pembrokeshire coast.

Acknowledgements

Thank you to all those kind people who gave me encouragement though they did not know me. Especial thanks to Mr Bradbury, a retired editor of the Birmingham *Sunday Mercury* who gave advice and encouragement and steered me gently in the right direction. Thank you Sir Adrien Cadbury, retired chairman of that famous firm and now its biographer, who explained how he had written his book. Thanks to Sir Frank Price, one time member of the Birmingham Watch Committee and Lord Mayor who gave personal advice, and to Mr Grinham, my old Sergeant, who wrote the Foreword.

Thank you Ron Hadfield QPM, our Chief Constable, who had kind words of praise for me and my efforts. Chris Morgan, author and tutor and the other staff at Northfield Adult Education Centre showed great interest and support for my venture. Also cheering me on where Lord Tonypandy, the late Harold Evans, Lord Howell, Michael Jefferson (late of D'Oyly-Carte Opera) and David Bloxham.

I must thank a large number of unamed "contributors" to the book who helped by stiring my memory of countless events over 27 years. They include serving and retired police officers, traffic wardens and lollipop people.

To each of you, thanks from the bottom of the size tens on which I trod for so long.

Foreword

I first met Roy Crompton when I was transfered to B Division of Birmingham City Police in 1952, and became his section Sergeant until my retirement in 1964.

His writings are little stories of every day (or night) happenings in the life of an ordinary copper, on the beat, on foot. It is a lot more interesting than rushing around in a car. Cars may be a bit more glamorous, but I can say from my own experience that there is nothing like being an ordinary copper, coming into personal contact with the public at all levels, something missing when in a car.

The Policeman on the beat comes across all sorts of strange situations which he must deal with, that is why I have said so many times that coppering is the greatest study of human nature that anyone can ever experience.

Roys's stories are true: some may seem farfetched and almost unbelievable, but having contributed to a few of them I can vouch for their authenticity.

It is these anecdotes that makes the book interesting and gives the reader some insight into what the man on the beat comes across. Nothing spectacular perhaps, but interesting.

E J Grinham
Handsworth Wood, Birmingham
14th November 1995

Contents

Introduction

For 27 years I was just an ordinary Bobby in Birmingham and the West Midlands. These stories are collected from my own experience or have been passed on by colleagues in the force or members of the public.

Names of characters, where given, have been changed, but all the figures are real enough. Some people may recognise themselves but nobody has been maligned by intent or accident. The only character who falls flat on his face due to some naivety or other is me. I was often in some minor trouble with colleagues or members of the public, who I always found most forgiving. Something which Joe Public finds very acceptable is a ready admission of mistakes. It was sometimes embarrassing but probably saved much later stress in trying to cover myself.

These stories are little studies of people and the small details of how we all react, feel and live, and they give an impression of how Joe Public thought about his local Bobby. Although they are all from my own experience, I worked in many areas over a long period and so to some extent they are a random cross section of Birmingham police experience. I hope therefore that this book will not only entertain you, but give an inside view on how the police in Birmingham actually worked between 1950 and 1977.

Finally, it is strange in retrospect that it should have been Birmingham. When I was looking for a job in 1949 I applied to my local force in Stoke on Trent, but they would would not take me on with a height of less that 5 feet 9 inches. I was 5 feet 8.5 inches. You must judge whether the missing fraction was good for Birmingham.

Roy Crompton

(1)

Something for the Sergeant

Kings Norton Police Station was a lonely outpost. One hundred
yards away was the roundabout on the modern Redditch Road,
but nearby Kings Norton Green is an ancient place. The
Cinema, shops and Old Saracen's Head are faced by a row
of houses to form two sides of a triangle. On the other side
is the graveyard of St Nicholas's church. Sometimes around
2.00 am an owl would hoot from the nearby trees. It could be
eerie.

One night at this dark time, a man got off a bus at the roundabout. Finding his way home past the Green, he saw a donkey
nosing and grazing. He pondered for a moment, then remembered the Police Station and lead the animal there without
much difficulty.

I was on duty alone and would be until about 6.00 am, so I
received a donkey. The animal seemed to be lost property and
would have to be kept somewhere where it would not come to
or cause any harm. At the time I could not think of anywhere
better than the back of the Station.

The building was shaped like a E without the middle stroke,
but with a wall across the back. In the middle was a patch
of lawn with borders. I could not get the donkey up the
steps into the front door of the Station, so I lead the way
round the back. The rescuer followed leading the donkey.
We went through the sergeant's yard and another yard to the
space I had in mind. We left the donkey with a bucket of
clean water and locked the gates. On the whole I felt that
I had done my best for the time being.

It did occur to me that the donkey seemed very wide. I
wondered about a foal, I wondered about malnutrition, I
wondered if I could be imagining it.

Having entered details of the man and the donkey in the Lost Property Register, I rang the RSPCA. The manager of the local home arrived at about 3.00 am, he might have been cursing under his breath. Looking at the donkey he told me not to worry and that someone would be along at about 9.00 am to collect it.

Apart from an occasional peep through the window into the darkness, I did not think much more about the donkey. When I handed over the Station to the early turn officer he had a quick look round, but did not go into the garden.

When I reported for my next duty at 9.45 pm I was surprised to find the Sergeant waiting. He asked if I was the lucky man who had taken in the donkey, but I did not need to answer because he knew.

"Did you look at it at all in those three hours?" asked the Sergeant.

I told him that I had looked from the back door but it seemed to be still and quiet. I must have looked puzzled; the sergeant's face was giving nothing away.

"Have a look outside with your torch", he invited.

In that pleasant little garden with its lawn and flower beds there was not a flower left. I was speechless. There was no explanation, but he knew that in the early morning I was in an awkward position, and he would probably have done the same.

"I got up after my sleep", continued the Sergeant, apparently enjoying the position, *"and when I opened the back door I knew something had happened. When I opened the gate I saw hoofmarks and I wondered who had eaten all my flowers."*

"Next time you bring an animal into my back yard", he added,
"would you shovel up the muck?"

"Sure", I answered. I thought he took it very well.

Docile Dog

Over many years in the police force I dealt with about ten cases of dog bites. Our working rule of thumb was that the dog was "allowed" one bite, for which we would caution the owner to keep the dog under proper control. An official record was made of the incident, so that if there was a second bite the owner could face a court appearance to show cause why the dog should not be destroyed. It is not so much that Parliament had licenced all dogs to enjoy one mouthful, but that an isolated incident might not give enough evidence to show the animal was dangerous.

Enquiries into these cases always involve getting a good description of the dog and the incident from the victim, and witnesses, and identifying the owner.

I had got as far as tracing the owner of a large, ferocious multi-coloured mongrel and called at his home in Rednal. The owner said that it was a peaceful dog and good with children, but it has been chased by children leaving school and become excited. In fact it had snapped at and bitten a little girl. There were two sets of teeth marks in her arm which had broken the skin, so she had gone to hospital for an anti tetanus jab.

The dog's owner was a middle aged man who clearly cared very much about animals. He kept repeating that the dog would not harm a soul and invited me to see how docile it was. I wondered why it was growling and baring its teeth while it strained to get free from the owner's grip on its collar. The dog did not like me. I sweated; it had already bitten two children.

How in these circumstances could I carry out my expected duty and write down a statement? The owner suggested that I sit at the dining room table while he kept the creature behind the kitchen door. I could write away for as long as I wanted, so long as he could read and alter the statement before signing.

Sitting down, I asked the relevant questions in a loud voice, and the owner shouted back above the continued growling of the dog. For twenty minutes I scribed away, recording every minute detail. I did not want to return for a repeat performance.

Completing the involved statement, I checked it, then pushed it and my pen under the kitchen door. The dog owner read, reread, then signed and returned statement and pen. I escaped, grateful for not being bitten. That was the last statement I took in shouts from a person in another room.

At the court hearing the magistrates ordered the dog to be put down. This was sad because the children at the school had actually liked it. They did not realised that it could be dangerous when excited. I realised too, that when I met the dog he had smelt my nervous perspiration, and this had made him worse.

Coach Stop

It was a dark and dismal autumn night and by midnight the streets were empty. First I patrolled my beat to make sure that the pubs had turned out and nobody was left to cause a fight or other mischief. Then I started checking properties.

Pershore Road in Stirchley was deserted. I had checked the shops and was continuing my patrol when I spotted a coach pulled up to the kerb. A few people got out and disappeared into a dark corner, and an odd thought struck me. I wondered if the coach had stopped for ... I hoped not. It occurred to me that there was no public toilet about.

Realistically, every coach outing has a problem as evening grows into night, and it is unwritten law that the driver must find a place to stop. But I could not imagine so many people wanting to go at once.

As I drew nearer to the coach I saw one or two people looking in my direction. Of course, I might be wrong and perhaps no such thing was happening. In any case, it would not be the end of the world. The problem was that if I caught sight of anyone satisfying their needs, men standing or women crouching, I was duty bound to book them for committing offences.

At the door of the coach I saw the driver who nodded and looked non committal. I looked straight at him, hearing a noise like a waterfall. What was I to do? Should I make a big fuss and take all the names and addresses, men and women, in the shaded angle of a factory wing?

There must have been at least twenty people in the dark away from the street lamps. It would take ages to get all the names and addresses. How embarrassing, with women adjusting their dresses.

(7)

If I ignored them they could well regard the law as soft. If my senior officer found out I would be taken to task. I was often criticised, I had to watch it.

I gazed straight ahead and slightly upwards, glad that they were all out of the light. Some 50 yards on I turned a corner, then stood for a moment. A man came up saying he would like a quick word.

"Look", he said, *"We fully realise that you could have booked us all and spoiled the whole day out, but for some reason you didn't. We are all most grateful, thank you."*

"Oh!" I replied, *"I can't say I noticed anything. Are you sure it was me who passed you?"*

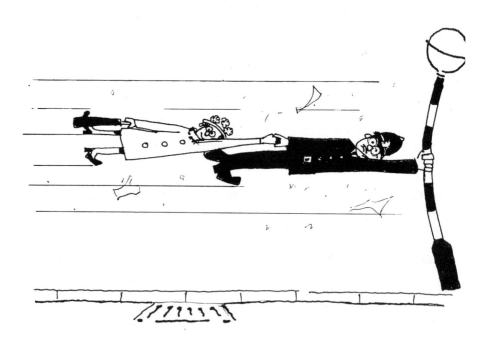

High Wind and an Old Lady

From where I stood outside Police Headquarters in Colmore Circus I could see the frail old lady had great difficulty staying on her feet. Apart from her frailty, she had to fight a mighty wind which blustered through the office blocks and buffeted people as they stepped round corners.

She must have been 80, and I became concerned when she stepped from the pavement onto this busy junction. She was having trouble keeping her hat on, and I was not sure whether the movement was deliberate or accidental.

I was worried, inaction became stressful, I strode decisively across the road. She could not hear my voice nor I hers. Holding her arm gently, I started to guide her across the road.

Ambling back to the pavement I had left a few seconds before, it seemed to me that the rescued lady was not as happy as she should have been. I spoke, I shouted, but my voice was gone with the boisterous wind. The lady seemed quite agitated, no - alarmed, as I escorted her to my base in the foyer of Police Headquarters.

"What do you think you are playing at young man?" she enquired distressfully. I explained what I had seen and why I had done what I had done. It did not seem to make the least difference, the lady continued complaining. Perhaps the least I said the better, but I did manage a profuse apology. This set off an outburst of anger and I began to feel very deflated.

A policewoman arrived and managed to calm the old lady. Eventually it emerged that she had been waiting for a relative on the street corner. Now because of my gallantry, she might have missed them. I offered my arm and she condescended to take it, but more willingly this time. I escorted the lady back to the corner whence I had removed her. She nodded approval. I was grateful for this at least and smiled, as much as to say. *"Good day madam."*

A elderly couple came up, but the roar of the wind made it impossible to hear anything anybody said. They and the frail lady started walking away, but as they went she turned round and waved gently. I waved back and thought I saw a little smile.

The Long Way Round

In those days, you got a day or a night off duty when you had completed seven shifts. On a weekday off I had been to see my parents and fiance at Trentham, Stoke on Trent. As a young, single man in the police I had to stay in quarters attached to the Station and eat in, so I had to return. And on that day I had to get back for the night shift at the old Stirchley Police Station.

Mum and Dad lived in the station, so I intended to catch a 7.00 pm train and change at Stafford. There would be a connection to Birmingham after a few minutes which should arrive in time for me to catch a bus and get on parade at 9.45 pm.

I ambled down the platform and crossed to the line. Soon the old steam engine hissed to a halt, carriage doors clunked open and people got out. I picked an empty compartment and nestled down into the corner; an overcoat over my knees gave warmth and comfort on this chilly autumn evening.

The train set off again, *" ...dee-dee-de-dum... "* pulling south towards Stafford. I noticed one or two passengers handing their tickets to the porter. They would be home soon, warm in bed just after I started duty. I would be going to bed when they would be getting up. But this was the life I had chosen so it was no use complaining.

I decided not to nod off on the twenty minute journey to Stafford. The train sped faster, " ...*dum-de-dum, di-di-di-di-dum...* ". It was most soothing, very soothing, very soothing indeed. "*Mustn't nod off old chap...* " I told myself. It was dark outside as I prized open my eyes to force myself awake. It would only be a few minutes.... " *di-di-di-dum, di-di-di-dum* .... ", steel wheels on steel track kept up a monotonous beat ....

I eased into wakefulness with a dry throat - I was numb. My thoughts were confused and it was dead quiet. I was in a quiet, dimly lit railway compartment and outside it was pitch dark. Pulling myself upright I stared at my watch. It was about an hour since I had left Trentham - in that case I had not changed trains at Stafford. Had the train stopped for a signal? I pulled the strap and the window clattered down to show me the greyish stone of a strange, silent railway platform. If only someone would appear. It was like a strange world with nobody there except me. Was I dreaming? Was there a fellow human anywhere? I had to know.

Stepping down to the platform I took one step forward then another. They echoed in the cold air, so I took a few more paces to convince myself that I was not the only one there. There nobody else on the train. At the front the engine was hissing steam, but there was nobody in the cab.

Then I saw the station nameplate - it had *New Street* written on it. No damn it, it hadn't. Nor was it *Stafford,* nor a new new station at Birmingham. It said *Rugby.* What in heaven's name did I want at Rugby? The terrible truth dawned. My train had travelled on from Stafford and finished at Rugby.

I walked further but stopped on hearing a man's voice behind a door. I knocked on it and a swarthy, middle aged,

uniformed man poked his face out. *"Yes boss?"* he enquired.
I must have looked worried as I shivered involuntarily with
sweat on my face. The swarthy man was quick on the uptake.
I asked him,

*"Where do I get the next train to Birmingham and what time
please?"* He answered,

*"You'll get a train back in 40 minutes from over that side.
It's the last one, so don't fall asleep or you'll be late for
duty. There's a kiosk on the bridge, if you want to phone."*
He smiled diplomatically.

I hurried to the telephone kiosk feeling embarrassed at being
such an open book that the railwayman had me weighed up,
but I was wearing my blue shirt and black tie. I wondered
what excuse I could give for falling asleep, for being in
Rugby, and for being late for night duty. I put twopence
in the slot, dialed the police station and a voice answered.

*"I'm on night duty Fred - fell asleep on the train and miss-
ed my connection. I'm at Rugby and can't get back for nights
on time. It'll be a bit late, like 11.00 p.m."* The old time
office man replied,

"Oh yes, then you'll have to get in when you can". What
else he could have said I do not know. Then he started to
roar with laughter; it was a great guffaw, he rocked with
mirth, then roared again. Recovering at last, he said,

"I'll pass a message on," and replaced his phone. I relaxed,
all stress gone.

At Stirchley Police Station I felt horribly guilty as I showed
myself and waited for a right rocket. But the night duty man
said quietly,

*"You've arrived. Do the front shops and the canteen. That's
that."* I completed my duty and no one said a word.

Crime and *The Gondoliers*

As part of my evening duty I was asked to give attention
to an evening's entertainment, an operetta at the Cadbury
Concert Hall in Bournville. In the days before yellow lines
many cars would park in Bournville Lane and I would
have to supervise.

There certainly were a lot of cars, but after the show
started things went very quiet. I patrolled up and down to
make sure no headlights were on and no windows open.

I decided to show my face to let the stewards know that I was
doing my job, and they invited me to stand at the back and
watch the show. An amateur company were singing Gilbert
and Sullivan's *Gondoliers*. Bliss, I have been an enthusiast
since childhood when my father was a principal in the local
group in my native Ormskirk, Lancashire.

It was a good performance - most enjoyable. I popped out
to stroll about from time to time, aware of the possibilities
of thefts and such like, but it seemed quiet enough. Then I
returned, enthralled, to *The Gondoliers*.

When the opera finished at 9.45 pm it would soon be time
for me to book off duty. I wished everyone a good evening
and was duly thanked for my attention. In fact they were so
pleased with my attention that I felt as though I had made
friends for life

I strode into the Station office to say, *"All correct Sarge"*.
Normally the answer to that would have been, *"Alright
kid"* and you would be off. But the Sergeant pointed to a
very irate man and his wife at the counter.

"Where's his stolen car?" enquired the Sergeant.

"Stolen car?" I fumbled. *"I've been all the evening at Cadburys. I was supposed to watch the street and give attention at the Hall, but..."*

"Yes young man, but this gentleman's car has gone from outside the Hall. What are you going to do about it?"

I was speechless, my expression of injured innocence must have been something to behold. Eventually I answered,

"I'll go and have a good look round for it".

After taking some details I disappeared with my bicycle. I was gone for an hour or so, but returned with my tail between my legs, defeated. The couple were still there but my shift, complete with Sergeant, had long gone home. I announced my negative result and was given most disapproving looks by all. I would have crawled into a hole in the floor had there been one small enough.

Details of the missing car had been broadcast to the City. All that could be done had been done so the two victims were taken home. They didn't look very pleased with the police force or me. Could anyone have blamed them? I went to bed not too pleased with myself either.

The couple got their car back next day. It had been taken by a joy rider but it was in one piece. A friend of mine who was a member of the male voice choir heard the story and I was never allowed to forget it.

Actually, there was a silver lining to this cloud because I did make some friends amongst the stewards at the Concert Hall that night. Liaison between the police and the Cadbury Factory was always good, but I wondered if my clanger had strengthened relations. I was told by a close friend that there was no doubt about it.

In the Dogvan

I was to collect the old van from its garage in the yard at
Steelhouse Lane, then meet the police Dog Handler at his
home. I had been taught to drive by the Police Driving
School but this was my first real experience of driving a
police vehicle alone. It was pitch dark and I was nervous.

The van had been left facing downhill at an angle to the
garage wall. That was a good start. It was three months
since my driving test in 1958, which I has only just passed.
How was I going to reverse uphill in the dark from that
awkward corner. I scratched my head. That helped. I
could not find a light in the garage.

Needing to do something, I groped into the driving seat.
Here it was even darker, like being in a cave. *"Shall I go
and fetch help?"* They would laugh me out of the police
force - it had to be done alone.

I revved the engine, found the gearstick somewhere behind
me, let go what I thought was the clutch pedal and prayed.
The mudguard crunched against the garage wall. I took a
deep breath, straightened the wheel and moved on inch by
inch, sweating freely. At last free of the wall, I stopped
and tried all the switches and knobs in the cab, everything.
Here was the light switch, and perhaps I should have used
it before. Sweat soaked my uniform.

Three quarters of an hour after starting the operation I was
out with a scratch on the van's front offside wing. I had
better report it or someone else would get the blame. That
was a good start to the day. I picked up the irate dog
handler an hour late.

We went to the Selly Oak Police Headquarters at Oak Tree
Lane, Bristol Road, and I managed to enter the yard to park

the van. The dog handler left me there with it. He said that if I sat quite still we would be perfectly alright. I didn't like this idea much because the dog had a vicious reputation, but the handler repeated" *Just sit still. I won't be a couple of minutes.* "

It was a memorable ten minutes. At first I did sit there dead still, sweating again. The dog got bored and came up close to sniff about my back, my side and my hat. I dared not move - I knew the dog could bite. I sat still, growing more and more uncomfortable.

A policeman came up and spoke a few words. I nodded. He smiled but the dog growled at him so he left quickly. I started to sweat again, I shouldn't have moved. The dog was licking my ear, and when I tried to shrug him off he growled. I dared not move. My ear off, I thought. I wished the fool dog handler would come back. God help me. My head bent further and further forward to escape the dog, but it follow- ed, licking my ear. Every time I moved, it growled.

With great relief I saw my colleague return. He saw what was happening, with me rigid and sweating, and just growled at the dog which retreated to whine in a corner. The handler did not leave me alone with the animal again and I have not forgotten that day in 30 years.

Young Artists

I was a very privileged person to be invited to visit the school in Lozells where my daughter supervised the six year olds. Most of the children would ask sensible questions, she said, so to oblige I donned my uniform from helmet to boots, with all the little things that made up my duty kit.

Walking quietly into the hall I reached the offices and looked hopefully over the frosted glass windows for the face I expected. Before I spotted my daughter, I noticed several drawings by children of their impressions of things they had seen. Most of my daughter's class was made up of Bangladeshi and Jamaican children whose parents came to Britain before they were born, and the pictures had a variety of Asian names scrawled on in crayon.

I remembered my old school at Ormskirk in Lancashire. It had dark rooms, smelly toilets, staff with very old ideas, including plenty of cane unless you were a favourite, dismal stairways, and strict discipline from a frustrated head-mistress. I was picked on.

This little school was quite old but had an atmosphere that gave it life and soul. You could not put your finger on it, but the feeling was happy. My older daughter, Janice, loves working there and I knew my visit would be memorable.

"Mr Crompton", called an authoritative voice, and a young lady ushered me into a little classroom. Janice was teaching and as I entered and gazed down onto twenty six curious, brown, bright eyed faces with mischievous grins.

Remembering the crayon pictures in the hallway I concluded that there were plenty of sharp wits at this place. I warned myself to watch out or some bright child would ask a question I could not answer. I was introduced as "Mrs Bickley's daddy", but had no idea I would give those little ones the impression that I did.

It seems that a milkman, a fireman, an ambulance man and one or two other "men" had been asked to pop in and answer questions. Janice prompted the children and soon lots of arms were raised. I did my best to satisfy them. The main subjects were my whistle, note book and helmet. They all looked at that very closely.

After some twenty minutes of questions and answers, I realised that many curious eyes were fixed on my right trouser pocket. The children did not want to give their curiosity away so I did not overdo it. Putting my thumb in the dangling loop, I swung my hand out and then inward in a circular motion, and pulled out my truncheon. As it is withdrawn, you grasp the handle.

There were whoops and smiles from those brown faces. My daughter Janice had seen this item many times as daddy had got ready for work. I held my "peg" up for all to see. Shrugs of embarrassment followed, and a comment or two such as, *"I wonder when I'll feel that?"* quietly or out loud, according to how shy the individual might be. There were a few looks of sheer amazement. Whatever impressions my peg made, they would last.

Some days later Janice called to say that the results were out and added lightly, *"You might like to come and see the pictures done after your visit, they're quite interesting."*

Entering the school doorway, I walked slowly towards the art. It dawned on me that the caricatures on those papers had some resemblance to what could have been a policeman with a very big head, helmet and badge. Several drawings showed someone blue with a large helmet on a small body. Most figures had matchstick arms and legs. But attached to each of the left or right matchsticks was a huge brown or black club, cudgel or tree branch. Several of the drawings had merit, others less so, but all gave the same definite impression of a figure in a big helmet with a very big club. Some of the helmets bore a large star, which I took to be my force badge. I could be proud of that, at least.

Bear in mind that the truncheon we used in Birmingham in those days was not more than 18" long and 1.5" at its widest. The children got the pictures out of proportion, but it was shockingly clear what had loomed largest in their minds.

Reporting later to Janice I said that whatever good opinions I might have had of myself in the past had certainly been dashed by her brood. It was obvious that the only things about a policemen which really mattered to the youngest members of our community was his helmet, his truncheon, and possibly his badge.

Biking with the Sergeant

Parade was over and the afternoon duty had started. The Sergeant said that he would join me on my beat as far as the British Legion Club in Pershore Road, Selly Park to check that all was well. Being a bit naive, I did not quite understand the meaning of such a visit.

We made our way to the cycle sheds at the back of the old Police Station, and a few minutes after 2.00 pm we were pedalling towards the Club, which was about a mile down the main road. I was on the inside nearest the pavement.

The Sergeant, in his early fifties, was rather eccentric; quite a kindly character but no one knew what to expect from him. I had no idea that the place the Sergeant intended to visit was not the Legion Club to which I was heading, though it was on my beat.

Cycling along that fine August afternoon I thought how good it was to be alive, happy that the Sergeant was showning me some attention apart from the usual criticism. We neared Selly Park Road, a left turn which led up a hill. Cycling on down the main road I was most surprised when the Sergeant wheeled left into the side road. Since I was riding on the inside it was more than awkward when he turned straight across my path.

We met with a thwack, his 14 stones to my 11. There was a thud of colliding bodies and the crash of meshing steel. I was thrown left into a heap on top of my bike. The Sergeant landed on top of me with his bike on top of him. We were both stuck. There was just a pile of policemen and bicycles, without helmets.

Some people from a bus stop came to ask if we were alright, and were we hurt. It must have been just as embarrassing for them. The Sergeant and I slowly extricated ourselves from the tangle. At last we stood upright and brushed ourselves down with our hands. We were dazed but none the worse.

"I thought we were going to the British Legion Club for some reason", I said almost apologetically.

"No." He regarded me with suspicion, *"You know I live the first on the right up there, don't you. I was taking you for a cuppa!"*

The last thing anybody expected in the police was for the Sergeant to take you home for a cup of tea. You certainly never expected such a stern Sergeant to act like that. I was introduced to the Sergeant's wife and for a few minutes we drank tea. I was still smarting from my bruises but they would serve as a reminder that the Sergeant was not to be taken for granted. When he said one thing he could well mean another.

Night Duty

As a naive young man of twenty four years, I felt that life was still full of promise, even though night duty did not put me in the spirit of jumping over the moon. But that is the time, I reasoned, when fighting crime and being alert is even more important than during the day.

Approaching midnight on a lonely beat means that most local inhabitants are either going to bed or scurrying home with that intention. Even a keen young copper can get envious, but he or she will be up at least six hours before doing the same. Your mind is alert, but it creeps and flickers from item to item; important things, petty things, to the bed you will not get into tonight, back to the odd lock on this shop door. Then you think of the other mile of shops on each side of the main road, making a two mile stretch of walking, locks and walking. Your eyes get sore with darkness broken by shop or street lamps, then as dawn breaks, getting used to the new light affects the pupils. It is unnatural but you have to get used to it. I calculated that in 27 years, I served 7 years of nights.

One night of endless doors and pools of lamplight I ambled down the driveway of premises in Pershore Road, Stirchley and tried the door. It was secure - no it wasn't, it opened. This was a shock. Now what to do, I asked myself? I could walk in and check around, but what if something was wrong? I rang the bell on the door of the flat.

I gave it a good press and seconds later a man's voice rang out on the midnight air,

"Yes, what is it?" I tried to keep my voice down because the nearby flats were occupied.

"Your door is unlocked," I called in a muffled voice.

"You'll have to shout louder. I'm a bit deaf… that's right …. DEAF. " He sounded just like the old radio comedian, Al Read.

"The premises are insecure," I bellowed.

"Don't shout or you'll have all the neighbourhood up," he snapped. Down he came and I motioned again to the door.

"Left it open have I. One of them will shut it", he said with a mischievous look in his eye. *"I'll see to it in the morning".* He gave me a strange look and I must have answered with a puzzled expression and said, *"They won't leave. "*

(22)

Who were they? I wondered, but dismissed the thought and carried on with my beat. *"Have a look when you come round again, they will be alright,"* he called after me as I walked away down the drive.

Some hours later I returned to check the door. It was still unlocked. Opening it, I peeped in and shone my torch round the black interior, then jumped back - all breath gone. I couldn't believe my eyes, but swallowed, took a deep breath and looked again. In my torch light I saw two pale female figures, faces upturned and quite dead. The light made them seem uncanny in the quiet and dark. I had to agree with the proprietor; who would rob an undertaker?

I had checked the premises again as requested and a second later I was off down the drive. That was *"They"*, I explained to myself. *"They can stay - I'm off"*.

Bruce and the Big Pull

I called in our Police Station at Longbridge to see if there was anything that pertained to my area, or for that matter, anyone else's. Police work is a world in which team spirit is nurtured and one is a cog in a big wheel. No copper can manage without the services that the force provides. In my day these included Control at the local Sub Division Station, the Central Control Room for immediate assistance, Ambulance Control gained from the Force Control Room, Police Dog, Fingerprints, Scene of Crime Officers, and many others - like dog kennels.

After a couple of minutes a man entered the Station Office with an enormous Alsatian. Or perhaps the dog entered with the man. To put it bluntly, it was a heaving mass of energy and the man was having quite a job to control it. Wherever that dog thought he might be going, he meant to go very quickly.

I gathered that the last place he would want to go overnight would be into a lost dog kennel at the back of a police station. I also gathered that one of the two of us on duty, the office constable or myself, would be putting the dog into it. Details were duly recorded by my colleague while while the dog hauled and strained at the leash.

The animal had been hanging about the finder's house for a couple of days. They had fed it, and fed it properly, then it would not go away because it did not seem used to such treatment. Now it was full of life and vitality. That might change overnight. The only food for dogs on hand in the Station was a bag of dog biscuits. The situation interested me.

Having completed the official entries and checked the collar for a name or address tag, which was not present, I said to the finder, *"I'll take the dog if you like. Do you want to see where it goes?"* No, he didn't - I was on my own.

I took the loop of the dog's leash, and as the man walked through the front door, the animal shot off after him. The loop was firmly in my grasp but this made things much worse, because there was no way I could resist. The dog was huge and lively and ran away with me on the end of the leash, Weighing ten stone in those days, I could not do a thing about it.

We soon caught up with the man who was walking rapidly along the main road. I bade him disappear quickly. He was so amazed that he offered to return with me to the Station and help me kennel the dog. I thanked him but declined.

I told the man to go round the corner out of sight, then tried to coax the dog. There were no police radios in those days, so I could not get help. Help with a mere dog, I said to myself. I thought of tethering it to a gate, then thought not. I tried patting the animal to get its confidence, but it kept straining its head to see where the man had gone.

When all else failed, I held onto the leash and dug my heels into the footpath. It was awkward as tugging a donkey that didn't want to move, one big tug of war. The trouble was, my team was weakening. How could a dog could be so determined? Perhaps I should let it go, but if I did there would be awkward explanations. I was often in trouble and could do without any help in that direction. Foot by grim foot my determination began to weaken the dog. After a heaving twenty minutes we arrived at back of the Station and an open kennel door. It was then clear that I had made an error.

The dog would not go into the kennel. It was not that I could not have shoved it inside a suitable kennel, but this one was too small. We started off again. I was deflated and beginning to feel the worse for the struggle.

I was tugging the dog down a passageway to the office again when the office Constable appeared.

"Hello," he said with a merry chuckle. *Where did you get to?"* I was just about to explain what I had been up to when he said, *"Someone has called in to say they lost a large Alsatian dog a couple of days ago. That might be the one."*

I gulped, heaved the dog the last two yards to where we had started off and met a man at the counter.

"Hello Bruce!" he said, *"Have you been a good dog?"*

"He's yours is he?" I said. *"You are lucky to get him back. He just ran away with me."*

"Yes, he likes his own way a bit," conceded the owner.

"What do you feed him with?" I enquired.

"He eats very little considering his size. Sometimes he runs off; then he eats anything he can get, I reckon."

I asked the owner if he could give his dog one good, regular meal a day to save the police the trouble of dealing with him. He replied,

"He only turns his nose up at tinned meat each evening."

Leaving the Station he remarked, *"He likes a fuss and a game you know!"*

Short Take Off and Landing

My beat covered a fairly wide area including Rednal, Rubery and Hollymoor, and it was accepted that if you had done the lightweight motorcycle course, you took out a machine. The water cooled Velocette's were quick, light, manoeuvrable and very useful in covering the roads in the wide open spaces of the suburbs.

It had rained heavily this particular afternoon. I had gone back to my patch at 7.00 pm and was motoring along Tessal Lane towards Frankley Beeches Road when something dazzling caught my eye, so I did not see the flooding. The water made the bike veer violently to the left, jump up the kerb at Elan Road and race on along a patch of grass. Meanwhile I was airborne, bottom and legs flying above the machine as it motored on. I wondered how long this could go on, and it must have been three or four seconds before my bottom landed back on the saddle.

I hit the seat with quite a shock, which caused me to loose balance so that I fell in a heap on top of the machine. It was covered in muddy water, but no dirtier than me. I wondered how to get the dirt off.

Riding the couple of miles to the Station, I took a hose to the machine which soon looked quite clean. So much for that part of the problem.

The mirror in the outside toilet showed that I was a real mess, with my coat, helmet and trousers all filthy. My face I wiped dry, but as to the rest ... I still had some time to go before finishing duty and I didn't want to look muddy. I thought of something rather ridiculous.

The coat, or mac, would not get too wet under the hose. My helmet might get soaked on the surface, but my trousers would only get wet at the lower end. Turning on the hose, I pointed the nozzle downwards, then stood there as water poured all down my uniform. A full minute later it was all done and clean.

My trouser bottoms were wet but my boots kept reasonably dry. When I booked off later nobody was any the wiser, and the motor bike was working. Later I discovered that what had dazzled me was the hospital floodlighting, which had been switched on as dusk fell.

Unthreading the Lady

One Sunday afternoon many years ago, I was the only police officer out on duty from an outpost station on Bristol Road South. Riding round my beat a Velocette motor bike, I called into the Station frequently to keep up to date with events. In those days we had no radios.

Calling in about 3.00 pm I found that a lady passing the Station had something to report. An elderly neighbour had called out to her as she passed her flat in nearby Mavis Road that she had a needle stuck through her finger.

I made off to the flat and looked through a window to see a face. But for some reason the elderly lady could not move, so she couldn't open the door to me. I tried other residents' keys and after a lot of messing about found one to fit. What was the best first aid treatment for a needle stuck in a finger? Could I pull it out? How had it got there?

The elderly lady looked very alarmed. She was sitting at a table on which stood an ancient, heavy sewing machine. The first finger of her right hand was where you would expect to see it while using the machine, but the needle was pointing right through her finger and jammed solid down the hole.

What possible way was there to get the needle out without doing more harm to the elderly lady. If I turned the wheel to raise the needle it would make matters worse. In the meantime I told the victim that everything was going to be just fine, and hoped that I was speaking the truth. She had been like that for an hour and a half and might have been hysterical had she not been used to a disciplined life.

I made up my mind that I could not, on my own, deal with the situation in any reasonable time. If the elderly lady collapsed with shock we would be in a worse position. Advising her to take a few deep breaths I left her for a few minutes with a neighbour while I got some help. From the nearby Station I called out the Fire Brigade, then returned to the flat. They came within three minutes.

It was fascinating to watch the firemen produce screw drivers and literally take the sewing machine to bits. In the end the little needle slipped out of the elderly lady's finger on its own, and she simply fainted with relief. An ambulance arrived and the crew calmed her down and took her to hospital. After treatment for slight shock and having the finger sterilised, she came home little the worse for her ordeal.

The Bournville Bubble Car

Being out alone at 3.00 am on a cold, dark, damp night was not my idea of peace and comfort, but I was not in Pershore Road, Stirchly for that purpose. I was the only policeman in that part of Birmingham on that early morning. The only other companion anywhere near would be in a patrol car answering emergency calls.

You kept your senses alert for any noise, say of breaking glass, or the clunk of a car door, as a would be joy rider chanced a free ride. The challenge was always present, wits against wits. It might happen that very night, or never. It was just luck if you caught a thief in the act, but the possibility kept you going.

I had passed a dark side street which led uphill and over a bridge, beneath which ran a railway and a canal. Nearby was the Cadbury's Bournville factory. That night gave evidence of a change in the wind because the sickly smell of caramel was stronger than normal. I was looking into a shop window for a moment when I became aware of a vehicle coming out of the road I had passed a few moments before. In the glass was the reflection of a man pushing a bubble car.

Turning round curiously, I saw that stopped in the centre of the main road was an old fashioned bubble car from the early 1960's. I do not remember the make but it was a two seater, the roof opened sideways and it was bright blue.

The man pushing the car was young with fair hair and a pleasant lean face; perhaps he could use some help. I asked him if he had trouble with the engine, but he replied in the negative. How polite the young chap was, he was no more than 24 years old. He had taken some little drink, but was certainly not at all tipsy. I was curious and suggested that if we pushed the car some 50 yards the next side road, it could be parked until he could remove it, or get it moved next day. We both pushed.

There was some drag which made it hard to move, but I went on pushing the car until we parked it. I suggested that the young man made sure the brakes were on and thought no more about it apart from asking where he lived. He said he was a male nurse and lived in quarters, but had got a bit fed up and decided to have a run round. It was then I did get curious, because I had suggested he check the brakes. He smiled and said he didn't know where to find them. I asked what he meant. He answered that he had no idea where the brake pedal was. Since the top of the car was open, this was odd. I felt the car body, it was cold. Surely he...? No, that was impossible, surely ...?

I chatted for a few more minutes. *"Have you got anything else you want to tell me?"* I asked amiably.

"As a matter of fact, I've pinched this machine," he said resignedly. I got the impression he was relieved to tell me.

"If you've stolen the car, how and why?" I asked, very puzzled.

"It was like this, you see," he explained. *"I've been out on the town and was having a walk round. I saw this on the forecourt of the garage in that road the other side of the bridge.*

(This was the corner of Mary Vale Road and Franklin Road, and the garage is still there.)

I fancied a drive in it because I never drove a car in my life. I haven't got a licence. I managed to open the top and get in, but I couldn't start it. After a while, pulling and shoving, I got it backwards onto the road and started pushing it along."

I cautioned him that "he was not obliged to say anything unless he wished to do so....". The garage forecourt was some 500 yards away on the other side of the bridge. How could he have pushed the car as it was, with the brakes on, over that steep bridge. He had to be very strong if he did it alone.

"How did you get over the bridge with this weight?" I asked touching the car.

"I got some of the Cadbury workers on their night break to give me a hand. They were a very friendly bunch, all four of them. They told me to get in, but I wouldn't. After pushing it over the bridge they left me as they had to get back. They were very nice. But they didn't see me push it off the garage forecourt."

I took the pleasant looking young man to the Station and charged him with taking and "driving" away the car, and being in control of it without a licence or insurance. He was fined and disqualified.

I passed the word to Cadbury's night foreman that staff should be careful when helping motorists with broken down cars. At 3.00 am a car could have a stolen safe in the boot. In fact I felt that I had been a bit of an accessory myself.

Strange Blue Light

After my break time I went to the backyard of Longbridge Police Station to get my Velocette motor bike for the next round of beat duties. With more than half the night's duty done I felt refreshed, despite the unearthly hour. It was a beautifully clear summer's night with a light breeze and a sky full of bright stars.

I rode away from the Police Station, took a left corner, carried on a couple of hundred yards then turned left again. Passing the hospital I saw a vast, blue circling ribbon of light coming down to earth very rapidly less than a mile away. In no way could I even imagine what it was.

Shocked and quivering, I tried to steady the machine and braked as soon as possible. Pulling it into the hospital entrance, I looked up at the sky again, but there was nothing, no blue light. Perhaps it was imagination. Being on nights has its peculiarities and maybe it was playing tricks on my eyes. I reviewed the experience. What I had seen was a blue or purple coloured light with silver edges coming down in a spiral, but a very quick one. Was it a shooting star? It did not shoot. Could I have seen a UFO.? Never - they didn't exist. How was I to know? There were reports one way or another every day of the week.

I pulled myself round after two or three minutes, then heard a long, low rumbling sound. Was it related to the mystery light? Was it something entering the earth's atmosphere?

I reported what I had seen at my Station and the Sergeant said quite simply, *"Nights aren't doing you any good either."* I smiled and walked away, embarrassed.

I was relieved to read a report in the *Evening Mail* that a police sergeant and a constable on night duty in Scotland at 3.00 am that morning had seen something strange. A blue colour with silver edges had come out of the sky and apparently landed no more than a mile distant. Despite a thorough search, they had found nothing.

When the mind cannot take something in, it may be best to forget it and turn to mundane matters. That way I felt safer riding my motor bike at night down, dark lanes and dismal streets in those lonely hours of the night.

Fright in the Night

Very early in my police service I patrolled the Victorian suburb of Ladywood. It was always an experience to go round the back of shops and factories. You could check on security and might sometimes disturb a thief in action.

It was the very early hours on a pitch dark night when I felt quite alone, and all I had for protection was a wooden truncheon and a set of handcuffs. Any self importance you might have felt was replaced at such times by apprehension for the dark and the unknown. And when you could not see beyond a yard or two without a torch, it was unknown. But the flash of a torch might warn a thief, so you kept yourself dark.

On these occasions I remembered that I was only 5 feet 8 (and a half) inches tall and weighed no more than 10.5 stones. I was not a big man, and it would not be an advantage if I ever caught a large violent one at the back of the shops. I never felt very sure about it and almost wished that I would find a big man. It would be better than imagining all the things that could happen.

I decided to go up an entry to check the backs of shops in a dark side street off Ladywood Road. I felt uneasy but did not know why, so I drew a deep breath and took one pace, then another, up the dark entry. As I advanced it grew darker By now I was all tensed up and could hear my heart pounding. Perhaps I was not alone. Imagination was playing havoc with my nerves and this would never do. I had to shine my light to convince myself that I was not scared stiff. I was, but why?

There was a loud thump followed by a *"ting"*. My heart leapt a yard, missed a beat, then beat ten times in a second. My throat was dry and I had stopped breathing.

There was a hiss, then a scream or whine. I stood petrified, wanting to run away from this sheer hell of not knowing what was going on. Then came a new sound from some yards away. It was a definite mew. I shone the torch to find cats eyes looking very radiant in the dark.

Reason returned, I felt a right idiot. I had disturbed the cat in a dustbin. As I crept past it had shot out and hit the lid, bounced off it onto another nearby, then shot onto a wall.

If things got like that again I would practise controlled breathing. This at least helps you to think in reality and see the things as they are. Making yourself tense by holding the breath only makes you worse.

On my very first lone patrol along Islington Row and Broad Street, I was not at all sure of myself. There were many shops to check, and I wondered what to do if I found a door open. This had never happened when I patrolled with other officers. I tried doors for some time and got used to it. It became automatic. There was nothing to it, it became a habit, it was almost a bore. I gained confidence. Complacency arrived. I was becoming quite experienced. I had been at it now for nearly half an hour. I could do this until the cows came home.

Bending forward to pull or push the next handle I saw a pair of shoes, right in front of me. Looking up I nearly jumped out of my skin. A tall man was looking down at me very calmly. He was very well dressed in a smart jacket and trousers. and I felt like apologising for my reaction. But the tall man didn't move. I calmed myself again - it was a tailor's dummy standing behind the glass door.

On another occasion I found an unlocked door on a shop somewhere in Northfield. Flicking on the internal light switch I saw a man lying flat on his back and looking very heavy in a coffin. I didn't expect that at 1.00 am and jumped, then left with a loud gasp. I had to do a bit of walking before returning to find the funeral director who lived above the premises locking the offending door. I was about to try and explain myself when he grinned.

"It happened before when this copper ran off shrieking". The funeral director seemed to be enjoying himself. *"He didn't bite you I hope?"* I did not answer, but after a calming second or two asked,

"Do you often have bodies in at night?"

"Oh Yes," he said, *"If ever you want a bit of company, just call in."* I half grinned and left.

Biking through the Flood

There was a close and menacing thunderstorm which seemed
to hang about all afternoon, throwing down frequent torrents
of water. I was on outside duty at the Police Station in Mary
Vale Road, Stirchley, which had a bicycle. Sadly, I had forgotten my cycling leggings. My pants were wet through from
the saddle so I was quite uncomfortable, but I had several
hours of duty left so I had to get used to it.

When I called in at the Station, a message came through about
a car at the far end of my beat near Pebble Mill. It was on
fire and might have been struck by lightening. Like a hero,
I set off again on my bicycle through the bucketing rain.

I rode off down the street, turned a corner and pedalled down
Bond Street. Turning into Ribblesdale Road, I realised there
was some flooding by the left kerb, so I braked to go round
it slowly. However my brake rubbers were very wet and I
was going too fast, so I splashed through the water and
caught the kerb a glancing blow.

It was quite enough of a glancing blow to knock me off
balance and I came off the bike. I finished up sitting in
the gutter with my bottom in the flooded road. Dazed, I
blinked, picked myself up and lifted the bike out of the
flood. Soaked through, I stepped towards the kerb, but
could not find the edge, so I tripped and fell into the
water again. This time my bottom was on the kerb and
my boots under water. I felt water seeping in over the
tops; it was deeper than it looked.

A lady came out of a house to ask me if I was hurt. I told
her I was fine and picked myself up again, watching where
I put my feet.

When I got to the blazing car, the flames had already been put out, and the cause was an electrical fault, not lightning. I returned through the downpour to the Station and gave details to the senior office Constable, who told me to put in a report. I sat typing for a while. It was not raining in the office. Absorbed, I did not fully realise what was going on, as water from tunic and boots dripped onto the floor.

The Sergeant came in, so I greeted him with the usual salutation,

"All correct Sergeant".

"Is it by gum?" he replied. *"Where did you find the car, in the River Rea?"*.

Bikers

On Bristol Road South was a forecourt which fronted about ten shops known as Tay's Corner. Here cars parked by a hot dog stand, shoppers passed the time of day, people did surveys for television and double glazing and bus passengers queued at the several stops. That was on weekdays. On Saturday afternoon they would scurry away around 4.00 pm, after deciding what to get for Sunday's joint, and the forecourt would be quiet. In fact, it became deserted.

As the local bobby I was on duty one sunny late Saturday afternoon, and was surprised to find no fewer than twenty motorbikes drawn up to the forecourt. Their riders were all dismounted, chatting and laughing. Some lads had girls with them, and there were one or two girl drivers. They had all removed their helmets and I suspected they had come a fair distance. One thing was certain, they were doing nobody any harm.

"All is well, I thought. *"What possible harm could these youths do? Of course, if some of the local residents saw such a gang, they might feel a little uneasy. They might get a little anxious. Should I have a little word in the bikers ears? No - why cause resentment for no possible reason?"*

A policeman's work is prevention and detection of crime, and preservation of life and property. Diplomacy is a useful asset and experience taught me that a wise action or word to an understanding ear can sometimes prevent a load of unnecessary trouble. I wondered how to get these youths on my side without a direct approach. I did not want to give the idea that I was a softie. A good way to get people's back up is to start checking documents on a car park. I had no such idea in mind.

I ambled down the road, nonchalantly walked into a public loo, then emerged. As I walked past the group I caught sight of a quite beautiful 650 cc motorbike, gleaming new and splendid. I took a step or two towards it and looked closely at handlebars, tank, brakes, engine and all.

As I was bent forward still admiring, I saw a pair of booted feet on my left and an adult male voice broke in,

"Is everything alright officer?" I thought for a second, then said in measured words,

"Oh yes, - it certainly is". I paused for a few seconds, glancing at the adult, youthful face of the man who had addressed me. I knew he was the leader by his self assurance and continued, *"I was just looking at this super machine."*

I noticed a flexing of the man's muscles and bulging of the chest. I had just passed him the greatest compliment anyone could possibly have done. I submitted to his pride smiling enviously,

"You're a very lucky chap". I added, *"You must be the envy of everyone."*

He told me all about his machine how many miles it did to the gallon and how many miles per hour. I could see he had the respect of all his friends. He was no fool and he knew how to drive. His machine was his badge of office.

Several nights later I was out on night patrol in the same road at around 11.00 pm. A passerby told me that two young Policemen were having difficulty with a gang of motor cyclists, so I thanked him and cautiously approached the same forecourt where I had admired a motorbike.

I was quite senior in service and did not want to come up to these two colleagues and make them look foolish. As I approached I guessed that the young officers had asked the youths to go, but a little rebelliously, they had consented to go in a minute or two.

Getting nearer I could hear a little bit of cat calling, the young calling the young. It was then I noticed that the young motorcyclist whose machine I had admired spotted me, and spoke to the others. They nearly all glanced in my direction 60 or 70 yards away.

I ambled on to meet the young officers and as I met them, all the young gang cleared off. The young man waved a gloved hand with a, *"Good night chief,"* and was gone.

The two young officers met me with a smile and a chorus of,

"You know them do you?".

"Not really," I replied, *"We have had words."*

Both officers bowed their heads slightly and I think I saw a couple of blushes, even in the lighting of the vapour street lamp.

Nature Prevails

It was a lonesome beat in the inner suburbs of the City, but at 1.00 am on a warm summer night in 1950, it was time to go to the Police Station for rest and nourishment.

I was then a young recruit. After leaving college at age 18, I did 2 years National Service, then 7 months at the Wedgewood Pottery near Stoke on Trent putting inches on my chest before joining the Birmingham Police. Green I was, and with little idea about life.

As I crossed the main road, I heard a noise as of running water from the side of a house. Perhaps it was a flood, someone's life may be in danger, I had to check. Water was running down the drive towards me, and I found that it was coming from a man leaning against the front of the building.

I pulled myself up to my full five feet eight and a half inches and tackled the man. He was urinating still and smelled strongly of beer.

"You are drunk are you not, and you are urinating, and it's going down onto the footway. That is a nuisance. It is an offence." I said sternly. He looked very disgruntled and I could see he was in a bit of a haze.

In my short experience, I had not shown much prowess in dealing with offenders, and I was not too sure of myself in handling a drunken man. I took his arm to help him back from the house frontage onto the footway, decided to arrest him for being drunk and disorderly and told him so.

At this point, he decided that it would somehow be better not to be argumentative, and to co-operate with the policeman. I was not aggressive and he had obviously enjoyed himself so we made our way to the Police Station. I did not enjoy the experience one little bit. The drunk was quite a weight to keep up, and supporting his considerable bulk was extremely awkward. As I struggled along he turned around, looked me in the eye and in a drawl which I found hard to understand, said something unintelligable. He tried again, but without success. Then in desperation, he started to drag me up another house driveway. I pulled him back, pointing out that it was not the way to the police station.

Finally, in a desperately pleading voice, he managed to form the words,

"Let me have a pee!", to which I stood with open mouth.

"You just had one," I reminded him.

"Let me finish my pee," he pleaded in desperation. I had no answer.

I hoped the Inspector or Sergeant was not watching. Here I was, in the gateway of a house at 1.00 am, holding up a drunk having a pee. I was glad it was very dark.

Sociable Climber

The Nurses Training Centre on Edgbaston Park Road is a Victorian building set in beautifully kept lawns. It was home to nurses on a starter course for the Queen Elizabeth Hospital, where they spent the first three months of the three year SRN course. In fact, this is where my sister started her nursing career.

At 11.00 pm the nurses were probably getting ready for bed in their first floor rooms. At night, owls could often be heard, making the grounds and building eerie. I was on patrol car duty with an experienced colleague and we were nearing the end of our shift. However it was busy and we had to answer a call which came over our radio. A trainee nurse had dialled 999 to say that someone was climbing a ladder in the darkness outside her window. She thought he might be after lead from the roof.

My colleague and I arrived minutes later, left the car on the roadway and quietly walked around the building, one on either side. It was very quiet and only the ghostly outline of the few trees broke the darkness.

Turning a corner at the back of the building, I saw a ladder leaning against the wall and narrowing to the roof two floors above. My colleague emerged and we looked up to see a dark humanoid shape near the top. It was still, but I could have sworn it had just moved down from the second storey.

We shouted up to the shape, I wasn't sure what it was at that juncture,

"You'd better come down here before you break your neck".

The shape climbed down. We were wary in case it tried to get away, which it might do if he or she had committed a crime. The shape was a young man in a light shirt and trousers, white sock and canvas shoes. He was no more than 20 years old, light haired, quite good looking and certainly no dullard. He looked puzzled, perhaps curious as to who had tipped off the law. He had nothing in his hands, not even a small rucksack to carry away loot.

He faced us nervously in the dark. I wondered if he had been en route to the roof or returning. He was almost certainly above the window when first spotted. Was that window to a bedroom...? My colleague went into attack,

"Well young man, what have you got to say for yourself? Are you going to tell me what you were doing up there or shall I tell you?" After a two second pause he went on,

(43)

"Alright then, it's very late, I'll tell you. You found a ladder in a garden and took it to climb to the roof to strip lead. You were caught in the act of climbing." He was bluffing, but it was as likely as not. The chap had given nothing away yet.

"Oh no, I've never been a thief in my life, I don't think I like the insinuation at all. Thieving has never been my style, I don't need to steal anything, though I don't know what my parents will say after this. They think I've gone for a few drinks. It's just a break from studying for my degree. I climbed up after finding a ladder at the bottom of the grounds. I saw the girl getting undressed with curtains open and fancied a peep. One girl pulled the curtain across, she must have told you chaps. I found the second one and was having a good peep when you called me. It was a good show."

"You are not obliged to say anything unless.," intoned my colleague.

"I know all about that," said the young man. *"I'm studying Criminal Law. I'm nicked aren't I?"* My colleague replied,

"I'm afraid so old chap. Conduct whereby a Breach of the Peace is likely to be occasioned." The student continued,

"I suppose that will mean a £10 fine and bound over for a year to be of good behaviour. It will have been worth it. It's a pity you had to come along and spoil it. You need an outlet from studying."

We marched him off and I told the nurse who made the call what was happening. She replied,

"I do hope he won't get into trouble. Thanks for coming anyway." I wondered what she had expected.

Lost Sheep Come to Town

Panda Cars and the Police radio system had not long been in use in the 60s, but they certainly kept you in touch with events on the patch. One day I began to hear reports of some sheep that had followed my leader out of a field on the outskirts of town, though I never saw any of the activity.

Various reports were transmitted to various officers that sheep were now in such and such a garden in the Weoley Castle area. They seemed to be shepherding themselves from one garden to the next along a road, then turning into another road, and presumably eating that out before starting on the next. Then the flock split into two or more groups. Things got more complicated by the minute.

I heard what I took to be the Controller, who would be a Sergeant, trying to hold back a laugh as he imagined possible reports coming in. It was getting a bit out of hand, having sheep wandering around the patch doing as they please. In any case, it is illegal allowing animals to stray onto the highway, so it was definitely police duty.

This episode went on for half or three quarters of an hour, with continuing reports of the sheeps' progress and damage done. The county police from whose area they had escaped were trying to find out who were the owners, hoping they

could collect them. Progress was being made, although it was hardly the kind of duty a city policeman expects. In fact, I began to think how ridiculous it sounded over the air.

Another Station Controller and other officers were calling in to take an interest in this exitement. All the time more sheep reports were arriving and being transmitted to officers. There was a certain amount of mirth.

I thought they would surely try to could keep the sheep penned into one willing householder's garden instead of allowing them back out. It was easy to talk however, as I was not dealing with the situation, and perhaps there was no such householder. I think this was the plan finally decided upon. Things were coming to a successful conclusion when the Policewoman who was the Control at the other Station on the Division despatched a unit car to deal with a completely different incident. It was at that point that the lady could not contain herself any longer.

She got a receipt of message response from the officer in the unit car and finished off the message with, *"Thank you Unit seven."* ... there was a small pause ... *"Baa"*.

Guards

In my first month or so in the Police Force, fresh from Training School, I was put in the care of an "experienced officer". That could mean someone with many years service, or somebody with a month more than yourself. The second could be the blind leading the blind, but with a lack of experienced men in the 1950s it was nobody's fault.

One evening I was being shown the patch off Bristol Street. My older colleague directed me to check factories on one side of the road while he checked the other. I tried the doors and locks along the dark street and I knew that if I found anything wrong, I was to shout for my colleague. I was still nervous and not sure of what to expect, since my worldly experience had been three years at college and two years on a quiet R.A.F. Station.

I tried the handle on one factory gate and it was unlocked. Then I tried the wicket gate set in the bigger one, and it was the same. I shouted to my friend but could not know that he too had found an unlocked door.

I shouted again, but this time there was a much barking from behind the gate. It grew louder and louder and louder, until it was a great ear splitting crescendo of barking and yapping.

Retreating, I went in search of my colleague, whom I found in another factory, and told him of my great discovery. We crossed the road and I pointed to the offending door. By then the dog, or dogs, had subsided, and the night was still and quiet until he touched it.

Instantly the yapping and barking was ear splitting, with goodness knows how many dogs throwing themselves against the inside of the door. My colleague turned white; even at

that hour when the face is white anyway, he turned white.
When he opened the wicket gate four, five, six or more dogs
tumbled out.

Suddenly the factory boss came out with a friendly smile and
called the dogs back. He had worked late and brought his
eight companions with him. They were all shapes and sizes.
He thanked us for our attention and invited us to have a
cuppa, which we declined as it was near to booking off time.

As we made our way towards the Station my colleague asked,

"Are your knees still shaking?" I admitted they were a little.
"Mine are rattling like mad." As I ruminated on what he had
just said I added,

"Put the wind up me .. really it did." I went on, *"They had
gone quiet after I found the door insecure. They were really
barking when I first found it open."* My colleague said,

"You mean you already knew ....?"

Off the back of the van

The school crossing lollipop lady had stopped a van for a
few seconds for the infants and juniors of Pershore Road
School, Selly Park. This was a busy spot on a main road.

The children had crossed, the crossing lady was walking back
to the curb and the van started off. Its back door was half
open ready for its next call and from somewhere on a heap
of piled up groceries, a giant cylindrical cheese came tumb-
ling down. It hit the road, bounced, and bowled down the
highway, coming to a halt yards from the lollipop lady.
Calmly she retrieved it and returned to finish her last few
minutes of duty.

After that, she tucked the large cheese awkwardly into the bosom of her white coat, mounted her little Vespa type motor bike, and whizzed off the mile to the local Police Station.

The Sergeant grinned wryly, then sniffed, and it dawned on him that the cheese could well go off pretty soon. Placing it in the fridge for a day or two was out of the question because it was too big. The prospects of locating the van or its owners, or of them collecting cheese, were extremely remote. It might have to be held as detained property for some time and that cheese did not look as if it would wait. The Sergeant logged the details from the crossing lady and relieved her of the burden.

The Sergeant mused on the possibilities, then sent somebody out to a grocer to ask if they could use a large cheese, and ascertain a reasonable price. The grocers had more cheese than they could cope with. After thinking it over for few minutes, the Sergeant asked someone to check whether the canteen had any cheese. They had not.

It depended on how many were in for an evening meal. Most officers brought sandwiches, having eaten before duty on the afternoon shift. I studied the cheese and decided against opening the sealed wrapping paper and breaking it into lumps to fit into the fridge.

If the canteen at Headquarters Divisional Station could use a some cheese we might get somewhere. I telephoned; they could use some that day. Our Sergeant sent a motorcyle rider with a wedge of cheese wrapped in greaseproof paper. There was still quite a large piece there left. As the men came into the Police Station for their evening meal, each was asked if their families could use some fresh cheese. Five of us had some and paid on the spot at the price advised by the grocer. Then one or two callers had varying amounts. By the end of the shift the cheese had not only reduced very considerably in size, but there was enough money to cover what had gone. The rest fitted into the fridge.

I think the Sergeant made a good salesman that day because nobody really wanted any cheese, and they only had it to help him. The word was passed that if anyone was short of cheese, there was plenty left in the Station fridge. Nearly everyone took some home, and for the next week I think they all had cheese on toast or other concoctions. The small portion left did eventually go off.

Nobody ever claimed the cheese, though we told the Central Lost and Found Property Office and enquired of a few local grocers. I suspect that when the van driver discovered that the cheese was missing, he would have put it down to a mistake when loading.

The incident was forgotten for a few days until the crossing lady entered the Station. At the time some chemical being used in the vicinity was giving off a powerful, pungent smell. When she addressed the same Sergeant who had received the said cheese from her, she remarked,

"What on earth's that smell, Sarge?" He answered with a wicked grin,

"I think it must be that cheese going off a little".

"Oh, really! You got rid of that, surely?" The Sergeant told her what we had really done with it, and added, *"You have a few quid to come in three months or so. Considering it fell off the back of a lorry, you will be alright."*

"You know," she said, *"it was hardly damaged at all when you think it fell on the road. You did well to sell it."*

"Needs must," said the Sergeant. *"It's surprising what you can do when you try".*

(50)

Polite Accident

In the early 1960s two of us were in one of the area cars used for answering emergency calls. Now they would be the "sandwich" fast response cars. In those days there were two cars on a big division as much as seven or eight miles long. The driver was usually an experienced policeman who had passed through at least three driving courses, including the advanced police course, and he was in charge.

The area had been quiet for most of that afternoon. We were parked at the top of the big hill topped by Frankley Beeches where the radio was more audible; we could hear messages from all over the Midlands. A call came that a street accident had occurred in Belgrave Road, almost in the City Centre. It was at the limit of our area and there was six miles of driving.

A street accident can be anything from a small collision to a catastrophe with a full turn-out by Fire Brigade and ambulance, but you do not always know what you are going to find. Time can be of the essence, but the police driver must still be safe as well as fast. I had not been with this driver before but was impressed with his performance. He showed every competence, steadiness and style. I took a lesson or two from him for a later day.

We covered the six miles through the housing estates, side roads, main roads and lanes of suburbia, then drew near to the City Centre. We headed for the junction of Belgrave Road and Pershore Road.

I spotted one car then another nearby, and it seemed they had crashed at this busy junction. There was no crowd, which is unusual. Crowds tell you that something serious has happened. They have to be got rid of as diplomatically as possible, but you may need the help of one or two people to get blankets or hot water, phone for an ambulance or something if you are tied up at the scene.

A small, fair haired, middle aged man around 50 years old emerged from the second car. He wore a shirt and jacket, dirty trousers and muddy wellington boots with the tops turned over. Another man got out of the first car. He was similarly dressed, as though both had not long come off a building site.

The small man seemed to sum up the situation quite well,

"I hit him sur", he said, straight to the heart of the matter. He had a very broad Irish accent. I thought at that point, as there had been an admission so to speak, that I should caution him.

"You need not say anything unless you wish to, but what you say may be used in evidence," I officiated.

"I hit him sur, fair and square I did sur. Where do I sign sur?" he concluded.

I had not yet put pen to paper but he was ready to sign. I thought, these building workers don't muck about. Two more rough, tough looking people I never saw, but they were two of the politest men I ever met. The paperwork was the least I ever did for an incident, with no witnesses there was nothing to record. These two thought they were doing the right thing, no argument, no words.

Smash & Grab

My personal radio crackled in Longbridge Police Station. The message was quite clear and to the point,

"Smash and grab", the operator announced calmly. *"The car has gone off towards the south. No other information available"*.

The office Constable put the Station telephone down. It was just before 2.00 am on a summer morning, when most people of sound mind and tired body are deep asleep. That is when thieves are abroad and most real coppers are alert for them.

The Duty Inspector had just popped in to keep in touch and was chatting to one of the men. I entered, and another colleague who had just finished a meal break joined me. Hearing the message the Inspector, a veteran of many years service, ordered,

"Right! Jump in the car outside. If there are any more, send them up. Let's go and get'em."

We were all seated in double quick time and the Inspector roared away in the opposite direction to the scene of crime, made a fast U turn into the other carriageway and headed towards the outrage. We reached the scene in two or three minutes.

In seconds we piled out in the darkness of the early hours to view a shattered shop window. The brick just inside showed the manner of breaking it. Tailor's dummies suggested what had been present in the shape of gents' suits. But one dummy seemed to be missing from the pattern.

The shop keeper or manager arrived and confirmed that the dummy was adrift, but probably nothing else. The information was broadcast to all Police Officers in Birmingham and West Mercia, then any officer calling in. Soon the message had rippled into Police Stations, cars, and bobbies on the beat throughout the Midlands. It used to make a cold thrill down the back of my neck just to think of it.

We left the shop manager to board up his window, so he could perhaps get a little more sleep before his busy day next morning.

Somebody had to start typing the paper work for the crime, so from bits and pieces given to me by the Inspector and colleagues, I started. What I could not finish would be done by the next shift at 6.00 am.

The M5 had recently been opened south of Longbridge and cruising Motorway Police spotted a Morris Minor on the hard shoulder. In the half light of the summer dawn, two young men were messing about with something in the boot. The officers pulled over to investigate, just what they knew not, but it made a few minutes rest from driving around in the dark.

As the two police stalwarts pulled in a few yards beyond the Minor, the young men jumped back into the little car and drove off. The police co-driver spotted something - long and white - sticking out of the boot.

"If I were suspicious," he announced, *"I would swear there was a corpse in that boot. "*

Jumping back into the police car, they sped off after the suspect Morris. They had just passed the Wychbold junction some six miles south of the Lydiate Ash slip road, when they saw it disappearing off the hard shoulder.

The officers stopped. In the new daylight they stood speech-less as the Morris Minor plunged down the embankment, a very white head protruding from the boot. They watched in awe as the car smashed through a fence, crossed a road, and seemed to run through another fence - no, that was an open gateway. The Minor charged on across a ploughed field and came to rest in the mud on the far side.

The two Police officers left their car without a word and reached the Morris Minor, puffed and muddy, three minutes later. The two young men still sitting in the car seemed dumbfounded, and out of the boot hung a tailor's dummy.

The Morris Minor was left clogged in the mud, the officers walked back to their car and passed the news via Birmingham Control to Longbridge Station. The Inspector took two of us beat men to Hindlip Hall, Headquarters of Worcestershire County Police, where two young thieves would be waiting.

It was well after 4.00 am on a brightening day when we picked up our smash and grab lads. They looked so young to our eyes, tired with the light after the darkness of the rest of our duty. The young men had enjoyed a good night out and nicked the car, which had not even then been reported as stolen. Full of courage, they had smashed the shop window and blundered off with the dummy.

The dummy went into store because you can only get so many people shaped objects into a car, and we all whizzed back to Longbridge to deal with statements, paperwork and routine.

The Right Lines

Sooner or later a beat policeman will be ordered to report to another Station, or another Division. This might be to make up numbers in case of sickness, or if there is a special job on, such as following up after some awful crime.

I found myself sent to Kenyon Street Station in Brmingham's Jewellery Quarter which has buildings dating back to the 18th century. This is craft manufacturing Birmingham at its traditional best. Even if the side and back streets contain buildings that are no longer in their prime, they do house some of the best small businesses, often with Jewish names, which are old and famous the world over.

In spite of all the gold, silver and gems being handled daily, the area is patrolled by the normal beat officers. Each business has its own security system and it is difficult to get in, with or without permission. The area is noted for its master craftsmen, all characters in their own right. They know their local Police well and you have to make yourself known and be accepted gradually. Cute people these jewellers, not to be taken for anyone's fools.

Late on a summer evening in the 1970s, I found myself alone in a part of this area I did not know, a rabbit warren of back streets. It was renowned for tough customers who were not troubled about giving the bobby a rough time after a few pints. I was very aware of this as darkness set in, but my main task for the next few hours was preventing crime. There had recently been a few attempts at breaking in and it was hoped that perhaps we could catch a thief.

I bumped into the local beat officers who went off in pairs to turn out the pubs. It would be unlikely if they returned to the Station without a fighting man the worse for drink, or maybe a fighting woman.

I found quite a few jewellers working very late, finishing special orders for the next morning's delivery. If I made a noise climbing a rickety stairway up to some doorway through which men appeared to be working (I hoped), I would use the security system to let them know who it was in case they rang the Police. I found one insecure office and rang in, but apart from this I began to realise I was becoming more alone as the hour approached midnight.

It dawned on my tired brain that it would be quite easy to get lost. I thought what it would sound like asking somebody the way back? What if I could find nobody to ask? Suppose I caught a thief and had to ask him the way to the nick. I felt a cold sweat at the back of my neck.

It was often a good job nobody knew what you were thinking. I feel sure this is why all police at some time or other wear an air of invincible confidence. They are not always full of the joys of spring, they suffer from stress, fear, even panic, and have to hold it down. I remembered my feelings when, as a recruit, I disturbed a cat in a dustbin, and when I was confronted by a tailor's dummy. Not every police officer completes their full 25 or 30 years.

It was approaching time to return to the station and book off at the end of a fruitless four hours extended duty. I found myself at a T junction on a main road, then realised that I had forgotten my street guide and hadn't a clue how to get back.

I hadn't seen a soul in the half hour since leaving the work-shop. How or who to ask? I didn't want to be late. I waited and waited and felt an utter fool. *"If I walked that way .... ?"* I might walk in the wrong direction. *If I walked that way? ....* Damnit, I couldn't make up my mind.

Then I heard the distinctive sound of a metal shod boot on stone, then again. Was it coming this way? Yes it was, and as the railway engine driver emerged from the gloom, I asked,

"Can you please tell me how I get to Kenyon Street Police Station?"

The robust and reliable veteran stopped in his tracks.

"You are standing at the back of it, actually," he confided, adding, *"But you have to go all round the block to get to the front, there's no other way."*

I thanked the railwayman and sped away to book off two minutes late. The inspector looked mildly baffled, probably wondering why this Policeman was puffing. I saluted and went to my car, remembering the diplomatic smile on the engine driver's face. I wondered how many Policemen he had directed back to their Station in the early hours of the morning. I have passed the spot where I stood lost at 12.55 am that morning and it looks quite different by daylight.